The Meaning of Politic

THE MEANING OF POLITICAL MYTH IN ERNST CASSIRER

CLAUDIU BACIU

Copyright © 2016 by Claudiu Baciu
All rights reserved. No part of this publication may be reproduced,
distributed, or transmitted in any form or by any means, including
photocopying, recording, or other electronic or mechanical methods,
without the prior written permission of the publisher, except in the
case of brief quotations embodied in critical reviews and certain other
noncommercial uses permitted by copyright law.

Contents

Ernst Cassirer's Understanding of Scientific Knowledge
7

Myth as Symbolic Form
20

The Myth of the State
26

Conclusions
39

References
45

Ernst Cassirer's Understanding of Scientific Knowledge

Ernst Cassirer (1874-1945) is considered, based on the extraordinary breadth of his work, one of the last great humanists. A true *Uomo Universale*, he mastered Einstein's physics, Hegel's philosophy, the Culture of Renaissance, Goethe's works, and the history of religion as well as the history of science. His method is a synthesis between Kantian and (in a somewhat paradoxical manner) Hegelian philosophy on the one hand, and the structural and functional thinking of science on the other. A protégé of the neo-Kantian H. Cohen, and considered one of his most important students, Cassirer further developed Cohen's ideas. So, although he was considered to be a Neo-Kantian, he was a special one. Cassirer had his own particular views regarding the science of nature and believed a broader general philosophical perspective was necessary. Despite this originality, many of his contemporaries considered him to be only a Neo-Kantian. Due to this, Cassirer remained largely at the periphery of philosophy, since the 1930s in Europe at least. Interest in his work was rekindled when others discovered that it expressed anticipation of structuralism and postmodernism.

Many of his books seem to be only historical works, presentations of writings and ideas belonging to authors of the past. Despite his immense erudition, Cassirer is not only a historian of ideas but also an original thinker for whom the appeal to the past is rather an opportunity to assess and acknowledge the contributions of his predecessors to the development of certain ideas or disciplines. For any problem he deals with, Cassirer first presents its history and different approaches to explaining it. In this way, he succeeds in not only giving a very accurate presentation of the problem but also in showing the manner in which other conceptions have formed over the course of time. We have to emphasize the particularity of his method, one which corresponds to his general views, such as expressed in his work *The Philosophy of Symbolic Forms*. Cassirer himself maintains that with his method, he is indebted to the Hegelian phenomenology, namely to a "science of the experience of the consciousness," (Hegel 1986, 596, as it was the first title of Hegel's famous work), that refers to a science describing the experiences that the consciousness (human spirit, in general) has to go through in order to reach its present stage. Cassirer's philosophy of symbolic forms implies this historical dimension because it is only through this that one can observe the progress and the materialization of a certain symbolic form. Historicity remains for Cassirer and for his contemporary thinkers, including Heidegger, a fundamental trait of the human being. Even though, in his case, such historicity seems to be paradoxical, especially taking into account Ernst Cassirer's Neo-Kantian thinking – because it is not easy to comprehend how the pre-eminence of science and logic (one of the main features of the Neo-Kantian conception) can be ranked on the same level and associated with the historicity of man.

In the debate at Davos, Heidegger criticized Cassirer for his Neo-Kantianism, explaining that this philosophical stream interprets Kant's work, *Critique of Pure Reason*, as being only an epistemological treatise (i.e., an attempt to establish a foundation for mathematical physics). Neo-Kantianism, according to Heidegger, would also consider that the only domain of culture which may be seen as being the true object of philosophy remains this type of science:

"One can understand the common feature of Neo-Kantianism, says Heidegger, only by reflecting on its origin. This origin is the embarrassment of philosophy when faced with the question of what is left to do for it in the total body of knowledge. All that seemed to remain was just this knowledge of science rather than of what there is. This perspective determined the entire 'Back-to-Kant' movement. Kant was seen as the theoretician of a mathematico-physical epistemology." (Hamburg 1964, 214)

On account of such an interpretation – to further understand Heidegger's words – all other domains of culture would be depreciated to a level of a gratuitous play of the human spirit. We would find true knowledge only within science, and the model of every truth would remain the scientific truth, which is a "universal" and "necessary" one, as in Kant. Cassirer's answer reflects his theoretical approach:

"The status of the mathematical sciences of nature is only a paradigm for me and not the philosophical problem in its entirety. There is one point, though, on which both Heidegger and I do agree and that is the central importance of the productive imagination for Kant. I was led to this insight by my work on the symbolic (forms). Imagination is the relation of all thought to intuition (*Anschauung*), a 'synthesis speciosa'. Synthesis is the basic power of all pure thought." (Hamburg 1964, 214)

Thus, we see that for Cassirer the problem area of philosophy goes beyond the sphere of mathematical sciences describing nature, even if these sciences represent a paradigm for the philosophy. However, the sense in which we must understand this paradigm is given by the last sentence, which expresses exactly the essence of the entire conception of Cassirer. For him, synthesis is the fundamental power of every thought, and the aim of philosophy is to explore this "basic power" of synthesis which belongs to the human spirit, in all the domains of its materialization. This program also continues the investigations of H. Cohen. Therefore, says Cassirer, "I do not look upon my own development as a defection from Cohen" (Hamburg 1964, 214), whom he regarded to be more than an epistemologist. Summarizing Cohen's intention of exploring that "basic power" of the spirit, an intention he developed throughout his systematic work about symbolic forms, Cassirer said:

"The primacy of activity over possibility, of the independent-spiritual over the sensible-thinglike, should be carried through purely and completely. Any appeal to a merely given should fall aside; in place of every supposed foundation in things, there should enter the pure foundations of thinking, of willing, of artistic and religious consciousness. In this way, Cohen's logic became the logic of the origin." (Habermas 2002, 42)

Cohen has emphasized that an understanding of the activity of consciousness must not be restricted only to the mathematical sciences of nature, as Kant has done. The unity of consciousness, understood as a unity of the cultural consciousness, has to also become the main research object of philosophy (Görland 1906, 15). Cohen saw the unity of consciousness, in the Kantian meaning, as a synthetic unity. He also held the view that the cultural unity of consciousness, which meant for him that human culture is the result of the synthetic act of the consciousness, must be investigated as a materialization of that unity. But what does this synthetic unity of consciousness mean? What does the concept of "synthesis," considered by Cassirer as being the "basic power of all pure thought," (i.e., of spirit) mean?

This concept comes from the Kantian philosophy, where it may be seen as an authentic cornerstone of the whole Kantian system. One knows that the Kantian philosophy distinguishes between the thing in itself and the phenomenon, and that, on account of this distinction, the concept of knowledge with which Kant operates is one which is valid only for the phenomena: we know the phenomena, says Kant, but not also the thing in itself. Our knowledge presupposes a matter of knowledge (sensations) and a form of knowledge (concepts). In the most general meaning, conceptual activity is seen by Kant as an ordering activity, whose object is the "manifold" of intuitions. However, this ordering activity presupposes a criterion: an instrument of operating which means that the undetermined manifold of intuitions can be arranged in representations, namely it can build a unity. Certainly, our representations do not appear chaotically in our consciousness. This composing is the result of a double-activity of the human soul: a) of the productive imagination, that arranges our intuitions in different concrete relations to one another as we see the result of this process in our current experience; and b) of the intellect, which produces the meaning of these representations. The "meaning" of our representations is the concept, and this is actually a function (i.e., the result of the activity of bringing a multitude of representations under one common representation):

"All intuitions, says Kant, being sensuous, depend on affections, concepts on functions. By this function, I therefore mean the unity of the act of arranging different representations under one common representation." (Kant 2, 1881, 60)

We may say that Kant was the philosopher who introduced the term "function" into the language of philosophical thinking. But "function" is only one aspect of the activity of the human spirit. Another aspect, one correlated with function, is "synthesis." Kant describes this as follows:

"In its most general sense, I understand by synthesis the act of arranging different representations together, and of comprehending what is manifold in them under one form of knowledge. (....) We shall see hereafter that synthesis in general is the mere result of what I call the faculty of imagination, a blind but indispensable function of the soul, without which we should have no knowledge whatsoever, but the existence of which we are scarcely conscious. But to reduce this synthesis to concepts is a function that belongs to the understanding, and by which the understanding supplies us for the first time with knowledge properly so called." (Kant 2, 1881, 68-69)

Hence, synthesis, as an act of the (productive) imagination, combines images, and builds from different representations a new one, as, for instance, from a succession of perceptions about a mountain the unique intuitive image of that mountain. The function of intellect means that this "manifold" can be recognized and comprehended as forming a single object: the mountain. Therefore, when Kant considers human knowledge as being a continuous process of bringing many different representations under a common one (i.e., as a functional unity that belongs only to the human consciousness), he believes that he has the right to consider human reason as not only being a pupil of nature, but also a true judge of it:

"Reason, holding in one hand its principles, according to which concordant phenomena alone can be admitted as laws of nature, and in the other hand the experiment, which it has devised according to those principles, must approach nature in order to be taught by it: but not in the character of a pupil, who agrees to everything the master likes, but as an appointed judge, who compels the witnesses to answer the questions which he himself proposes." (Kant 1, 1881, 368)

This concept of knowledge is not a simple mirroring of nature; it excludes the understanding of knowledge as an activity reflecting the external environment of a human being in his inner consciousness. Human knowledge is not a result of reflection, but is the result of construction, albeit not just arbitrary construction.

Without a doubt, in the discourse of the *Critique of Pure Reason*, the mathematical science of nature occupies a privileged place, and for good reason. Comparing metaphysics with other disciplines which pretend to offer a knowledge of reality, Kant observes that in metaphysics we have to deal with a disagreement between authors, while in the sciences we encounter agreement between researchers who work in that field. Being himself a great admirer of metaphysics, Kant's intention was actually to discover what makes this agreement possible in science, and to subsequently apply that condition to metaphysics. Such agreement meant that all scientific statements are "universal" (i.e., accepted by all members of the scientific community) and "necessary" (i.e., admission of truth is the result of a rational constraint which cannot be eluded). Kantian construction, therefore, is based on the fact that Newtonian science, associated with mathematics and logic, has encountered no major transformation throughout history.

According to Kant, knowledge becomes true knowledge only when it succeeds "to enter on the secure path of a science" (Kant 1, 1881, 369). However, such disciplines in his time were only Newtonian physics, mathematics, and logic. The scientific character of these disciplines was based on their deductive nature, explained by Kant as being rooted in the transcendental structure of the intellect. To him, pure intuition and categories determine an object and thus draw the horizon from which this object must be investigated. The fact that logic has not encountered any major modifications since antiquity made Kant believe that supreme functions of the intellect – functions which were identified by him with categories – are given by the types of judgments that were discovered by Aristotle, as several representations synthesized under a single, common one.

Kant affirms there is an unchanging structure of knowledge, a pure and universal reason which is present in all human beings. Self-knowledge of this reason is accomplished not directly but through its activity. On the one hand, reason discovers its true identity on the basis of its errors, and on the other hand, on account of science developed through history. Only by reflecting on such science, is reason understood to be an a priori faculty that possesses certain "innate" principles uniting (synthesizing) all content that comes from outside the human spirit. Kant affirms that only because there exist such "innate" or a priori principles which determine the synthesis of the manifold of intuition, can we explain the possibility of scientific predictions. These predictions are in fact exactly a recognition of the synthesis which is permanently operated by the intellect and imagination, only on a subconscious level. All scientific judgments express explicitly the earlier unknown (i.e., subconscious) operation of the human spirit. The discovery of "the secure path of a science," namely of the operations of the human spirit, is accomplished during the course of history by means of attempts, successes, and failures, as normally happens with all human actions. The historicity of man is in this sense an important component of Kantian philosophy.

For Cassirer too, as we have seen, the idea of the Kantian synthesis and the idea of the (intellectual) function remain fundamental terms. Actually, due to the fact that these two notions represent different aspects of the same act, they are often used, even by Kant, as interchangeable concepts. For Cassirer too, knowledge has a functional character, namely meaning the act of bringing a manifold of representations under a common one. Unlike the case of Kant, such activity no longer expresses the subconscious operations of the human spirit, rather it is an activity by which the object itself is created. In his work *Substanzbegriff und Funktionsbegriff*, Cassirer introduces a fundamental distinction for the entire twentieth century. The major theme of this writing is the process of building concepts, both scientific and common. Cassirer starts his investigation by describing Aristotle's manner of explaining this: our concepts reflect the true resemblance that exists between things. That is the reason why we speak about a correspondence between concepts and real things.

"For Aristotle, at least, says Cassirer, the concept is no mere subjective schema in which we collect the common elements of an arbitrary group of things. The selection of what is common remains an empty play of ideas if it is not assumed that what is thus gained is, at the same time, the real Form which guarantees the causal and teleological connection of particular things. The real and ultimate similarities of things are also the creative forces from which they spring and according to which they are formed. The process of comparing things and of grouping them together according to similar properties, as it is expressed first of all in language, does not lead to what is indefinite, but if rightly conducted, ends in the discovery of the real essences of things. Thought only isolates the specific type; this latter is contained as an active factor in the individual concrete reality and gives the general pattern to the manifold special forms. The biological species signifies both the end toward which the living individual strives and the immanent force by which its evolution is guided. The logical doctrine of the construction of the concept and of definition can only be built up with reference to these fundamental relations of the real. The determination of the concept according to its next higher genus and its specific difference reproduces the process by which the real substance successively unfolds itself in its special forms of being. Thus it is this basic conception of substance to which the purely logical theories of Aristotle constantly have reference. The complete system of scientific definitions would also be a complete expression of the substantial forces which control reality." (Cassirer 1923, 7-8)

The Aristotelian ontology dominated western thought until the end of the Middle Ages. In it, our concepts reflected real substances, those which were effectively *in re*. Between knowledge and reality, there was no insurmountable wall as there is in the case of Kant. This understanding of knowledge gives ancient and medieval science a qualitative character, unlike modern science, which has a quantitative one. Ancient and medieval science tends to grasp the inherent substance of things, and not the relations between them. Even more, mathematics, considered by us to be the science of these relations, was considered by Aristotle as an obstacle on the way to this understanding. Nevertheless, states Cassirer, in mathematics and geometry we deal with a different type of concept building. Mathematical concepts do not reflect outer realities, and the numbers and geometric forms cannot be considered to be such reflections. On the contrary, in mathematics, we encounter a real *Setzung*, or a creation of concepts. The same thing happens in the modern science of nature. Here, science that separates itself, only with difficulty, from substantial conception, namely from a self-understanding as a knowledge of the real substances, finds its theoretical method using certain conceptual constructions, as a means by which it can investigate reality afterward. Due to these fundamental concepts, scientists can select from a multitude of aspects of reality. We find such selection in every science, says Cassirer. This selection takes place even at the level of our common perception. Hence, we encounter reality only while starting with the use of a previous concept about the thing that we are about to encounter. This is the new functional model for understanding knowledge supported by Cassirer, a model in which reality is given to us according to the concepts that we already know:

"Without a process of arranging in series, without running through the different instances, the consciousness of their generic connection – and consequently of the abstract object – could never arise. This transition from member to member, however manifestly presupposes a principle according to which it takes place, and by which the form of dependence between each member and the succeeding one, is determined. Thus from this point of view also it appears that all construction of concepts is connected with some definite form of construction of series." (Cassirer 1923, 15)

"The connection of the members is in every case produced by some general law of arrangement through which a thoroughgoing rule of succession is established. That which binds the elements of the series a, b, c, ..., together is not itself a new element, that was factually blended with them, but it is the rule of progression, which remains the same, no matter in which member it is represented. The function F (a, b), F (b, c), ..., which determines the sort of dependence between the successive members, is obviously not to be pointed out as itself a member of the series, which exists and develops according to it." (Cassirer 1923, 17)

And finally:

"Every mathematical function represents a universal law, which, by virtue of the successive values which the variable can assume, contains within itself all the particular cases for which it holds. If, however, this is once recognized, a completely new field of investigation is opened for logic. In opposition to the logic of the generic concept, which, as we saw, represents the point of view and influence of the concept of substance, there now appears logic of the mathematical concept of function. However, the field of application of this form of logic is not confined to mathematics alone. On the contrary, it extends over into the field of the knowledge of nature; for the concept of function constitutes the general schema and model according to which the modern concept of nature has been molded in its progressive historical development." (Cassirer 1923, 21)

The transformation of the concept of function in Cassirer's thought, compared with Kant's concept of function, means for him that the conceptual recognition of the "subconscious" activity of the soul is a process which is treated for itself and not in relation to a background which is external to knowledge. If we relate Kant's conception to Aristotle's substantialist conception, we can say that Kant internalizes the substantialism of Aristotle, and that "substances," although they do not exist anymore *in re*, only *in mente*, are still seen as existing to some degree separated from knowledge, namely in the sphere of the subconscious acts of the soul. Therefore, Kant can give a new definition for truth as correspondence between our knowledge and subconscious acts of the soul:

"We do not know of things anything a priori, except what we ourselves put into them." (Kant, 1, 1881, 372)

But what we put into them are the general conditions of the experience, those conditions that make possible our relationship with the objects:

"We say that the conditions of the possibility of experience in general are at the same time conditions of the possibility of the experience themselves, and thus possess objective validity in a synthetical judgment a priori." (Kant 2, 1881, 139-140)

Kant internalizes the conditions of the possibility of objects and admits the existence of humans who have a universal transcendental structure (the totality of conditions that make possible our experience with the objects). For Cassirer, such a structure no longer exists. The idea of a universal human being presupposes a universal manner of concept building, namely, by grasping the resemblances between them. Kant further admits that we develop concepts as Locke has explained it, starting with the simplest impression, and evolving into a more general concept through gradual abstraction:

"Such an investigation, writes Kant, of the first efforts of our faculty of knowledge, beginning with single perceptions and rising to general concepts, is no doubt very useful, and we have to thank the famous Locke for having been the first to open the way to it." (Kant 2, 1881, 77)

Certainly, this method does not explain the objective validity of our concepts, but it explains their history, being thus only a response to a *questio facti* (Kant, 2, 1881, 77). By changing the perspective, Cassirer renounces the Kantian assumption of the primacy of the unreflected experience, that is the premise of the existence of an experience about the objects, which must first be given to us in order that we may reflect on it and thus build concepts about the objects that belong to it. His argument is that any science (true knowledge) does not proceed in this way but instead "posits" (builds) certain concepts, thereby opening a certain horizon of objects, and a certain plain of objects, which have not existed earlier and apart from that concept:

"The individual thing is nothing for the physicist, but a system of physical constants; outside of these constants, he possesses no means of possibility of characterizing the particularity of an object." (Cassirer 1923, 148)

Science, based on its fundamental principles, creates a domain of objects that will be investigated during the development of that science. Contrary to Kant's thinking, these principles are no longer conditions of a universal experience; rather they are the conditions of a special experience (i.e., relationship with objects) particular to that field of science, an experience that is not reducible to any other kind of experience. Thus, even the term "phenomenon" changes: phenomena are no longer the objects conceptually determined by the intellect or objects that we find in all of our experiences, but now every scientific domain encounters a special kind of phenomena. Using its own principles and concepts, a science creates a network which permits it to create particular types of phenomena, i.e., the objects that it investigates are thought of and described as being derived from those principles:

"It is only owing to the fact that science abandons the attempt to give a direct, sensuous copy of reality, that science is able to represent this reality as a necessary connection of grounds and consequents. It is only through going beyond the circle of the given, that science creates the intellectual means of representing the given according to laws. For the elements, at the basis of the order of perceptions according to law, are never found as constituent parts in the perceptions. If the significance of natural science consisted simply in reproducing the reality that is given in concrete sensations, then it would indeed be a vain and useless work; for what copy, however perfect, could equal the original in exactness and certainty? Knowledge has no need for such a duplication, which would still leave the logical form of the perceptions unchanged. Instead of imagining behind the world of perceptions a new existence built up out of the materials of sensation, it traces the universal intellectual schemata, in which the relations and connections of perceptions can be perfectly represented. Atom and ether, mass and force are nothing but examples of such schemata, and fulfill their purpose so much the better, the less they contain of direct perceptual content." (Cassirer 1923, 164-165)

Since science conceives every object starting from its principles and schemes, induction, a fundamental process of scientific inquiry, is not a paradoxical and incomprehensible generalization. This induction isn't conceived any longer as an extension or generalization of specific observations that are extended to the entire class of scientific objects. Rather, every induction, says Cassirer, is founded upon a certain way of conceiving the individual case. That is to say, that from the beginning, induction projects in each particular case content that transcends it radically, transforming each as an exponent of an ideal rule. The reality is that the process of adding new cases through empirical observation actually confirms the rule which existed from the beginning in the mind of the researcher, adding to or building on our knowledge, and not merely leading the researcher to discover a new rule:

"The logical act of 'integration' which enters into in every truly inductive judgment, thus contains no paradox and no inner difficulty; the advance from the individual to the whole, involved here, is possible because the reference to the whole is from the first not excluded but retained, and only needs to be brought separately into conceptual prominence." (Cassirer 1923, 248-249)

In this way all the objects that a certain science investigates are not only phenomena – a concept that emphasizes only the difference between the content of knowledge (which only "appears" as the concept expresses it) and reality –, but are also "symbols," entities which exist only because they express an immanent rule:

"Each particular member of experience possesses a symbolic character, in so far as the law of the whole, which includes the totality of members, is posited and intended in it. The particular appears as a differential that is not fully determined and intelligible without reference to its integral." (Cassirer 1923, 300)

Thus every science generates its own symbolic field. Moreover, the human being is, on account of his entire activity and life, as Cassirer said later, an *animal symbolicum* (Cassirer 1944/1972, 26). That means that in each domain of his activity the human being encounters objects only because he thinks them by means of a certain formula, of a certain scheme of understanding, of a certain sense: because he thinks them in a certain way. Therefore, the existence of a layer of experience that could precede thinking and its instrument, the judgment, is denied by Cassirer:

"The fact that there is no content of consciousness, which is not shaped and arranged in some manner according to certain relations, proves that the process of perception is not to be separated from that of judgment. It is by elementary acts of judgment that the particular content is grasped as a member of a certain order and is thereby first fixed in itself." (Cassirer 1923, 341)

Concluding that perception, the elemental act of the human consciousness, is pervaded by a symbolizing character, and that each of the different sciences have a symbolic approach, irreducible to other factors (thus being asserted that there exists an irreducible plurality of symbolizing acts), Cassirer may now generalize this idea of a symbolic character by conceiving man in general as a symbolic being, who, through his entire activity, projects around him an autonomous network of meanings. Cassirer does not develop this idea in his writing of *Substanzbegriff und Funktionsbegriff* but acknowledges that he discovered it while working on it (Cassirer 1, 1977, V).

Myth as Symbolic Form

We find the development of the previous idea in his *Philosophy of Symbolic Form*, that represents the systematic work of Cassirer as an expression of his philosophical conception. At the beginning of the first volume of this work, Cassirer maintains that his writing about substance and function must be developed by showing not only the way in which symbolic activity of man takes place in the sciences of nature but also in other domains of human existence. In other words, it was necessary to investigate the different modes by which man encounters the "world," and their articulation. Also, it was necessary to present the specificity of those modes and their irreducibility to other faculties of the human spirit. In general, says Cassirer,

"Under symbolic form, one should understand every energy of mind through which a mental content of meaning is connected to a concrete, sensory sign and made to adhere internally to it." (Cassirer 1956, 175)

The term of "symbolic form" has three meanings in Cassirer's philosophy. Firstly, it signifies the relationship established between the symbols of a certain domain, Cassirer using in this sense terms such as "symbolic concept," "symbolic function," or the "symbolic character" (*das Symbolische*). The second meaning of this term concerns those domains of culture where these symbolic relationships are materialized: myth, art, religion, language, and science. Finally, "symbolic form" means the fundamental categories of thought including space, time, cause, and number, which acquire a specific form in each of the domains mentioned before (Hamburg 1949, 77). We have seen earlier, that the term "symbol" is conceived by Cassirer as it is used in science, namely as a sign that stays in a predefined relationship with the totality of signs. The symbol is not so much a sign that is related to something real that is substituted by this sign, as it is a sign that receives its meaning only on the grounds of its intrinsic relationship with the totality of signs in which it is included. Cassirer would then subscribe to Husserl's idea, that:

"…to signify is not a type of a sign in the sense of being an indication" (Husserl 1901, 23).

Hence, the sign has no existence by itself, but it is produced by a law or principle of generation, which produces that totality of signs where each particular symbol is included. This principle of generation, which is precisely the "symbolic form," founds the great domains of culture. But each domain has a specific symbolic form, or its own law of generation (Cassirer 1, 1977, 12). Only from a formal point of view can we talk about a universality of the symbolic form, because all domains of culture presuppose the existence of a certain act relating their contents. However, the act of relating that belongs to a domain is completely different from the act of relating that belongs to another domain, making these domains irreducible with others. Language, as symbolic form, is not reducible to a simple transformation in a linguistic sound of an emotional reaction caused by reality. Even if the linguistic sound is also such a reaction, the fact that human beings, in the primal stages of their development, have different emotional reactions before different aspects of reality, proves the existence of a selecting activity regarding the contents of reality, a selection, for Cassirer, that is possible only on the grounds of a certain function. In the same way, the contents of myth are not reducible to the language (as a certain direction of myth interpretation has believed), or to other faculties of the human spirit. Myth is the result of an autonomous symbolic activity. Thus, says Cassirer, the philosophy of symbolic forms does not search the categories of the consciousness of objects only in the intellect but assumes that such categories must act everywhere, from which chaotic impressions, a cosmos or typical "image of the world" shall be built. Such images of the world are possible only by means of specific acts of objectification, i.e., a transformation of simple "impressions" in representations which are determined and well-articulated in themselves (Cassirer 2, 1977, 39).

The relation of a concrete symbol (of a certain symbolic content) to reality is always mediated by the principle of generation specific to the domain where that symbol belongs, a principle that realizes the synthesis of all of our "impressions". The "indication" of the real thing is possible only on the grounds of that mediation. Therefore, the indicated real thing is, from the beginning, an exponent of the symbolic function and not an autonomous existence.

As we have seen, myth is also a "symbolic form". Thus, mythical thought cannot be a simple "distorted" reflection of a reality that exists in itself, nor can it be the expression of man's fear before reality, or the expression of a rationality that does not yet possess adequate means – these are only two of the modes in which one has explained the origin of myth. Such interpretations would reduce myth to other faculties of man, depriving it of specificity. Cassirer considers that his theory is not an anthropological interpretation of myth, but a "philosophical theory" of it (Cassirer 1946, 4). Starting from the Kantian distinction between *questio juri* and *questio facti*, we may say that for Cassirer, the philosophical theory of myth explains its truth content, while the anthropological interpretation tries to describe the way in which the different representations – evolving from a general structure of man's faculties – have appeared. Such interpretations presuppose that there exists a permanent nature of man throughout history.

The symbolic dimension indicates not only the building of a functional unity of meaning, but it is also a process of objectification. The term "objectification" comes from the era of German Idealism. We find it in the works of Goethe and Fichte, but most of all in Hegel. Here we meet the idea of the objectification of the Absolute Spirit, which has an existence that objectifies itself by means of its many creations, that is to say by means of its activity. In Cassirer's philosophy, where the assumption of such a universal Spirit does not exist, objectification means only that a certain content of consciousness becomes an object of it. The fact that an emotion objectifies itself means that it becomes an object of the consciousness. This emotion is now given to consciousness as an object, and now consciousness is able to apprehend and to know it. But the objectified content is not identical to the supposed content that would exist before objectification.

"The expression of a feeling, says Cassirer, is not the feeling itself – it is emotion turned into an image. This very fact implies a radical change. What hitherto was dimly and vaguely felt assumes a definite shape; what was a passive state becomes an active process." (Cassirer 1946, 43)

Thus, the perception, when it is objectified into language, acquires a different kind of reality. It becomes an object and is given to consciousness as an object. On account of this objectification, perception is no more what it was in a supposed pre-linguistic state. But objectification, as transformation into an object, materializes itself according to the functional laws of the domains where it takes place. The appearing object does not build itself spontaneously, in the absence of every kind of conditioning, rather, it builds itself starting from the conditions that make possible (i.e., intelligible) an object in the concerned domain.

"In language we objectify our sense perceptions. In the very act of linguistic expression our perceptions assume a new form. They are no longer isolated data; they give up their individual character; they are brought under class-concepts which are designated by general 'names'. The act of ‚naming' does not simply add a mere conventional sign to a readymade thing – to an object known before. It is rather a prerequisite of the very conception of objects; of the idea of an objective empirical reality." (Cassirer 1946, 45)

We may extend this description of linguistic objectification to all sorts of symbolic forms. Each of them, in the very moment in which they take over a certain content and objectify it, subject this content to its specific concept of object, and thus confer on it a meaning that has not existed before, removing its individual, particular character. By becoming an "object," that content can be now known better and better, and its features can be articulated in an increasingly complex way. For instance, starting with the investigations of Usener, Cassirer affirms that the divinities of the developed pantheons evolved from original deities that were indeterminate, and appeared instantly as "momentary deities" (Cassirer 1953, 15). They were, in Cassirer's opinion, rather peculiar emotional states that were later described as divine presences. The determination and assignation of more complex qualities to these primal divinities take place by means of experience, it also implies the historicity of human beings. Actually, "momentary deities" are grounded in a layer of mythological thought which was earlier than structured religion (personification of the divinity), being grounded in the representation of *mana*. This representation is a category of mythical and religious thought, namely that "form" (Cassirer 2, 1977, 96) which allows the realization of a unique type of human experience as religious experience. As a primal representation of mythical thought, the *mana* representation means a "wondering" (Cassirer 2, 1977, p. 99), and indicates that a certain thing is extraordinary, and draws suddenly the attention to primitive man. But unlike animals, this qualitative prominence of the thing leads not only to fear or curiosity about it, but at the same time represents the threshold of a new spirituality (Cassirer 2, 1977, p. 99). Thus the *mana* representation builds the core of the category of "holy", the fundamental category of religion. During the development of the religious life of humanity, the world divided into two spheres: the Holy and the Profane, the latter containing those objects which do not provoke an intensive emotion. The object which is first perceived as *mana* gradually acquires a number of features that build into a more clearly articulated representation of deities. Between the building of a religious pantheon, and the constitution of the empirical world of objects, there is an incontestable analogy. In both of them, says Cassirer, we can observe a transcending of the stage of isolation of the immediately given thing; we can observe that man understands all individual existence as being integrated into a network that forms a totality (Cassirer 2, 1977, 100-101). On account of this integration, different perceptions do not remain on the stage of an "aggregate," disorganized mass that has no order, but advance gradually to the condition of a "system," or a multitude, that has an inner organization (Cassirer 2, 1977, 101). Hence, objectification means for Cassirer the act of integrating into a determined form of an undetermined impression. In science, this would be in a "conceptual" form. This integration in a form is not accidental but is realized according to the specific logic of the respective domain. Thus any of the symbolic forms are seen neither as a true copy of reality nor as an arbitrary creation of the mind. Such a symbolic form has an internal logic. It materializes itself according to an "order of foundation," or *Fundierungsordnung* as described by Max Scheler, according to a synchronic and diachronic determination of meanings. Once objectified, all contents affect all the future experience of the individual human being and of mankind in general (Cassirer 2, 1977, 235).

Myth, as with all the symbolic forms, is the result of a sui generis way of man's relating to reality. We may only describe this way of relating, and how it develops in its own horizon, but we cannot discover the "causes" of its apparition. Myth is an autonomous world, and as in the case of Kant, who says that every attempt to determine the origin of the world leads us to dialectics of reason, i.e., to a theoretical impasse, so all attempts to explain the myth by means of other capacities of the soul annihilate it and make incomprehensible the ubiquitous presence of one of the most important spiritual realities of human history. Only by recognizing its specific character as symbolic form may myth be seen as staying in continuity with other manifestations of man, and may contribute to a better understanding of him. A reductive understanding (in this sense) of the myth is unable to explain its return to the political scene in the twentieth century. If myth is understood only as an expression of the original fear of man before nature, or only as a primitive form of rationality, grounded in images, then the recourse to mythical thought (rituals, magic language, etc.) in the twentieth century, an era of science, one of the most important results of the evolution of the human rationality, becomes absolutely incomprehensible.

The Myth of the State

From the foregoing explanations, we may understand that the title of Cassirer's last book means in no way that the state would be a myth, namely it would have only an illusory reality, and encourages us a certain utilization of the term "myth." This peculiar utilization means the understanding of myth in the course of the history as the "Other" of Reason; myth was always considered as a type of interpretation of reality, contrary to the rational interpretation of it. The first who saw myth as an infantile, naïve interpretation of reality were the ancient Greek philosophers. But we must not believe that reason appears suddenly in history. Reason, undoubtedly, is a dimension of the human being completely different from mythical thought, but its appearance and impact on history were possible only due to the inner evolution of mythical thought. Only because myth has evolved from the primitive representation of *mana* to more complex representations about reality, that is to say to a more clearly articulated religious conception following a dialectical process (in the Hegelian meaning of the term), was it possible to arrive at a certain understanding of it as being inferior to the rational interpretation of reality.

Cassirer says that in the evolution of language, there are three stages: the first stage of language only mimics reality; the second stage is an expression of analogies; in the third stage, language becomes a symbolic expression of reality. During the first stage, mimic of reality, we encounter the belief that the language and its components copy reality or are believed to be an immediate expression of reality. For example, when an object provokes fear and this fear externalizes itself through a certain sound, this sound is then understood as being the thing itself. There exists at this level a complete identification of the word with the thing. The word is not seen as being separate from it. At a second level, the sounds of the language, although seen as existing separately from the thing, are considered to have the power and the capacity to replace that thing. It is only on the third level there appears a consciousness that the linguistic sound, the word, is a sign that we use for the thing. We observe how, in the course of this evolution, a critical consciousness evolves from the entire identification of the word with the thing to the consciousness of the fact that this word is only a sign for the thing. We encounter the same evolution, says Cassirer, in the domain of myth and mythical thought. If, in the beginning, every mythical creation was considered as being reality itself, then gradually, mythical consciousness was transformed into a religious consciousness, a consciousness in which there exists an understanding that reality (in this case the divinity) and its representation are absolutely different. The representation being only a symbol of divinity (Cassirer 2, 1977, 285), a symbol that vaguely expresses the transcendent reality of the divinity that it signifies. Only by reaching this third stage of evolution of mythical thought, is the critical faculty of the human thought sufficiently developed to understand that mythical images are projections of the human mind and not expressions of reality itself.

Cassirer's intention in writing *The Myth of the State* is to explain how it was possible that myth received such great importance in the political discourse, action and thought in Europe, and in particular Germany, during the first half of the twentieth century. This phenomenon is not accidental according to Cassirer. It can be understood only if we consider the history of political thought as having the structure of a symbolic form, namely as a domain where functional relationships unify the diversity of reality. In this case, the synthetic principle that permits such integration is precisely the act of conceiving the political phenomenon. At first glance, *The Myth of the State* seems to contain only a history of political thought. However, we must emphasize that the historical dimension is necessary for the analysis of every symbolic form, i.e., the systematic character of its analysis presupposes the presentation of its historical unfolding. We have seen that a symbolic function attributes the original sense to a certain content, and integration of the manifold opens the "inner horizon" with meanings that are increasingly complex and rich. So, for instance, myth does not remain at the level of the undetermined representation of *mana*, but evolves in the direction of a more exact specification of the content of that representation, starting from the division of reality in the spheres of the Holy and the Profane, and continuing with the specification of profiles of the "momentary deities", until the last stage of religion, monotheism. But in all this evolution, the category, or "symbolic relation" or "symbolic function," that was for the first time objectified in the *mana* representation sustains and develops itself.

The symbolic function that founds political thought is the conceiving of the human being as a social being, namely a being that acquires its own way of existence only inside of society. Political thought is described by Cassirer as being a part of a process of rationalization that began with ancient Greek philosophy and lasted until modern times. This process of rationalization has, at its core, the gradual elimination of explanations that are grounded in divine intervention in the natural and human order of things even though the process began in antiquity, and lasted until the end of the nineteenth century. The beginning of this process consisted in a reinterpretation of the meanings of myth. This procedure accompanied the evolution of every symbolic form, as we have seen, from the mimetic stage to the symbolic. The sophists were the first to affirm that myths do not have immediate meaning but must be comprehended in an allegorical (symbolic) sense. But such an understanding gives explanation neither about nature, nor human beings. If myths are only metaphorical expressions of certain truths, then it raises the question about from where we receive these truths, and what kind of being they possess. The understanding of man becomes a theoretical urgency. Socrates, according to Cassirer, was the first to recognize this and considered that one can say nothing about myths until there is no knowledge of man.

Socrates had no political conception, however, on account of his theoretical interrogation regarding the nature of the human being, he compelled that philosophical thought be oriented towards the investigation of the social nature of man. Political conception happens in Plato's philosophy. Plato recognized for the first time the indissoluble connection between society (i.e., social organization), and individual soul. He recognized that an imperfect organization of society and dominance of corruption lead to perversion of the individual soul that belongs to that society (Cassirer 1946, 63). The same holds true in Plato's critique of mythical thought. In order to build a society which leads to a harmonious soul no longer corrupted by a corrupt society, a certain conception about divinity is necessary. It is a conception that we do not find in myths where we actually encounter only expressions of human traits.

However, the "Idea of Good," as a new and legitimate representation of the Deity, may lead man to a true "Republic," where individuals can develop harmoniously (Cassirer 1946, 66). From the point of view of the objectification theory, we may say that in Plato's dialogues the idea of an existence of a "political sphere" is for the first time objectified, and that there we encounter the first understanding of the power of politics and its importance in the life of individuals. Here one notices a "functionalization" of the idea regarding the existence of a political reality, the opening of a new horizon that will leave its mark on the future evolution of political thought. The opening of such a horizon means introducing a set of problems, and it establishes a certain axiomatic system, inside of which all future problems will be resolved. This political sphere presupposes, as an essential condition, the responsibility of man, a responsibility that was impossible during the epoch of mythical thought, where the individual has no control over himself and his thought, and where he remains in a Kantian state of minority of reason. Plato's state is built from citizens who have a homogeneous soul, a soul educated by means of principles that are in unity with one another and which are thus able to induce a homogenous effect in man's soul. A traditional mythical conception, says Plato, is not able to build a homogeneous soul, but only a divided one which possesses only contradictory impulses that never reach the stage of a real unity. Plato's ethical interest sustains his political conception. Happiness, which is the supreme good for an individual, cannot be attained randomly, but only in a "rational" way, namely through a rational following of the Good. Reason is a capacity that can be developed only in the context of a well-organized society. Cassirer gives the following synthetic description of Plato's conception:

"Of all things in the world myth is the most unbridled and immoderate. It exceeds and defies all limits; it is extravagant and exorbitant in its very nature and essence. To banish this dissolute power from the human and political world was one of the principal aims of the Republic. Plato's logic and dialectic teach us how to classify and systematize our concepts and thought; how to make the right divisions and subdivisions. Dialectic, says Plato, is the art of dividing things by classes, according to their natural joints, and not trying to break any part after the manner of a bad carver. Ethics shows us how to rule over emotions; how to moderate them by virtue of reason and temperance. Politics is the art of unifying and organizing human actions and directing them to a common end. Thus the Platonic parallel between the individual soul and the soul of the state is by no means a mere figure of speech or a simple analogy. It is the expression of Plato's fundamental tendency: the tendency to unify the manifold, to bring the chaos of our minds, of our desires and passions, of our political and social life into a cosmos, into order and harmony." (Cassirer 1946, 77)

During the Middle Ages, states Cassirer, the Greek philosophical conception, which is one of contemplation of eternal but impersonal truths transforms into a Christian conception, where the fundamental focus is that of the knowledge of God – a unique God – that no longer has an impersonal character but is depicted as a person. For Christian thinkers, in spite of how important ancient Greek philosophers were for their theoretical synthesis, the Jewish Prophets remain a major source of inspiration because in their writings one encounters a personal God. The revelation of the personal divinity (undoubtedly a mythical idea) surpasses rational thought and Greek intellectualism (Cassirer 1946, 81).

For instance, the Platonic Forms have become Ideas that belong to a divine Intellect, in whom the human intellect participates. Even if all themes of Greek antiquity are present in the writings of Christians, they acquire in this way a new, religious dimension. Man is reinterpreted from the perspective of his fundamental relationship with a God who revealed himself in history, and all his traits brought into light by the culture of antiquity are now reinterpreted with this new dimension. The fundamental idea that sustained medieval thought as formulated by Augustine was that in all the domains man has access to the truth not on account of reason (as viewed by Greek philosophers) but immediately, on account of God's revelation. Therefore, in antiquity, if reason or human thought possessed the main role, then in the Middle Ages this role was attributed more to faith:

"Reason left to itself, describes Cassirer the medieval conception, is blind and impotent, but when guided and illuminated by faith it proves its whole strength. If we begin with the act of faith we can confide in the power of reason, for reason has been given to us not for any independent use of its own but for an understanding or interpretation of what is taught by faith. The authority of faith must always precede the use of reason." (Cassirer 1946, 95)

Another aspect that medieval thought receives from antiquity is stoicism and its conception of the equality of man. This equality is founded on the principle that reason is present in all human beings, and also based on the capacity of man to educate himself in an ethical sense. This legacy is important for Cassirer, in that he says the medieval theory of the state is based on two postulates: the contents of Christian revelation and the Stoic conception of the natural equality of man. (Cassirer 1946, 106)

Thus, we see that the mythical vein is not abandoned in medieval thought. It acquires only a new form. In Plato's philosophical discourse, we encountered both a polemic against myth and a use of mythical means. On the other hand, in medieval Christianity, myth was an expression of a faculty opposed to reason, given primacy since religion and faith were considered to supersede all human reason.

Later, opposing thought between the conception of the ideal state (City) of God and the real state was founded in a mythical representation: the original sin. On account of this original sin every political institution was doomed to be imperfect:

"Here was a definite mythical element that could not be openly attacked. To doubt the fact of the original sin was impossible for any medieval thinker. On the other hand, the dogma of the fall of man obviously defied all efforts of dialectic thought. It was impenetrable and recalcitrant to rational explanation." (Cassirer 1946, 110)

Only in scholasticism does reason begin to free itself from domination by faith, and in Thomas Aquinas, we find a distinction between the two domains: the one of grace and revelation, and the other of reason and nature (Cassirer 1946, 111). This separation also affects the conception of the state. The state is no longer thought of only in connection with its ideal and transcendent model, a model that the temporal organization strives to attain, without actually succeeding in history. The same state is now thought of from the perspective of the concrete rationality of political acts and its organization. The rational organization of the society is actually proof of man's freedom. The emphasis is set now, not on the impossibility of attaining the ideal model, but on the power of reason to orient itself in accordance with this model:

"Despite the Fall, therefore, writes Cassirer describing the conception of Thomas Aquinas, man has not lost the faculty of using his forces in the right way and thus of preparing for his own salvation. He plays no passive role in the great religious drama; his active contribution is required and is, indeed, indispensable. In this conception man's political life has won a new dignity. The earthly state and the City of God are no longer opposite poles; they are related to each other and complement each other." (Cassirer 1946, 115)

With Machiavelli, the rationalization of political thought added a new feature. The first effect of this rationalization was a break with the medieval idea of a hierarchical organization of society (Cassirer 1946,

135). The tradition of a hierarchical social system was rooted in the cosmological conception of Aristotle who stated that the first cause of the Universe was divinity in the quality of an "Unmoved Mover," whose action propagates through the sky of "the fixed stars" over the entire world. The Middle Ages had thought of the world as being divided in a plurality of ontological planes, i.e., being ontologically heterogeneous. This model is also applied to the state, which is considered as having a divine origin, and also to the church. The leader of the state was the emperor, and the leader of the church was the Pope. Machiavelli considered that the state or "principalities," cannot have any divine origin. He observes empirically the mode of building such principalities in his time and comes to the conclusion that to attribute them to divine origin would be blasphemy. Machiavelli, on account of his realistic conception about the state and "political man" (a conception based both on the observation of his epoch and of the past), represents the most important attack against the medieval conception of state and its divine origin. In other words, it is the most important attack against the religious conception of the state.

The separation of the theological context that earlier framed theoretical meditation about the state is a part of a wider process that, according to Cassirer, comprises all the domains of culture. At the end of the Middle Ages, there existed a clear "intellectual line of demarcation" (Cassirer 1946, 130) between the Middle Ages and the Renaissance. In science, Galileo promoted a conception grounded on a different foundation than theologicy. The same was also true for Machiavelli:

"Machiavelli does not follow the usual ways of a scholastic disputation. He never argues about political doctrines or maxims. It is enough to point to 'the nature of things' to destroy the hieratic and theocratic system." (Cassirer 1946, 136)

Machiavelli realized in political thought what Galileo later realized in his cosmological conception: he eliminated the idea of hierarchy, of different ontological plans. The laws of motion are the same everywhere in the universe, and man is conceived in the same way by Machiavelli, no matter whether he is on the top of the hierarchy or at its base. Machiavelli presents the phenomenon of power deprived of its religious content, in the same way as science investigates his object, because it is not the moral and theological aspect which is important for the examined phenomenon, but the law that establishes it and its structure. Machiavelli is, from this point of view, an exponent of the new spirit of the epoch, a spirit oriented mainly towards this world.

Despite this conception with its profound rational elements regarding a universal human being, Machiavelli introduces in his discourse a mythical representation of Fortune. But unlike the medieval conception of Fortune, where it was only an agent of divine, absolute power, Machiavelli admitted that Fortune represents only a part of a cause that leads to a certain historical result, the other part being attributed to human will and power. In this manner of introducing this mythical agent of Fortune, Machiavelli operated with a profound sense of secularization, admitting that man is able to build, to a certain extent, his own destiny.

Another form of spirit that Cassirer presents is what we may call the science of politics from the seventeenth century, that considers not only that there is a universal human nature, but also that we can work out a "mathematical" science of the political domain. This was a science described in accordance with Galileo's science of nature model, and which presupposes certain metaphysical assumptions, such as the assumption of a universal human nature that may be known in the same way as the scientific principles. It is self-evident and is thought of in line with the canons of the mathematical science of nature, as a "substance" endowed with certain laws of manifestation. We see here a new moment in the process of secularization, where theological and mythical elements become more detached from the philosophical discourse about politics (Cassirer 1946, 164).

The transfer of this new science into the domain of political theory leads to the apparition of the theory of the social contract. Here, human beings are seen as being united in a state, on the grounds of the social contract. The state is no longer the result of divine intervention, and no longer has divine origin as it was considered during the Middle Ages, but also, it is no longer founded in an arbitrary way through the rational-technical methods of the Machiavellian Prince. Now, the state is interpreted as arising according to historical and rational laws as individuals renounce many aspects of their will – by means of a social contract – to impose the reality of the common will, the expression of which is the state. The idea of a multitude of individuals freely giving up their will in order to create something superior (the state), is rooted also in the ancient conception of stoicism. However, Cassirer shows that in the seventeenth century there was a revival of the stoic humanist ideals of antiquity. This revival represented stoic conception as applied to political theory: if all men are conceived as being equal, and having the right to act freely, it is possible to deduce the existence of a state from their accord, i.e., from the idea of a social contract. All the characteristics of the state may now be deduced on the grounds of this premise, as interpreted by Hobbes (Cassirer 1946, 174). The Enlightenment brought no important modification of this interpretative model. Philosophical interest was now oriented not to the discovery of new ideas, but to materialize these political ideas. The Enlightenment was not so much interested in political theory, as it was in political life (Cassirer 1946, 176). This is expressed by the fact that one of the most important thinkers of the eighteenth century, Imm. Kant, recognized the priority of practical reason when compared with theoretical reason.

Romanticism was a criticism of the Enlightenment, particularly for its lack of interest in history and myth. According to Cassirer, the Enlightenment was profoundly interested in history, but this interest resided in practical teaching that we can acquire from the study of history; thus, showing once again its practical orientation, whereas Romanticism was interested only in history for the sake of history itself, and in "superior necessity" which dominated it. The Romanticists' interest in history is thus a metaphysical one. The opposition between Enlightenment and Romanticism also exists with respect to myth. If the Enlightenment considers myth only to be a product of a past era of the human spirit, a product that has no value for the present day, an expression of superstition; then Romanticism considers myth as the major product of human culture (Cassirer 1946, 183). Interest in myth actually expresses the interest that this era had for poetic and "magical idealism," an idealism that finds one of its most authentic expressions in the work of Novalis, *Heinrich von Ofterdingen*. During this period of time, we see a passing from the era of reason to the era of imagination. Fr. Schelling was the first to elaborate a philosophy of mythology, where myth, as a true product of the spirit, finds its theoretical legitimization. Thus, with Romanticism, myth returns to the forefront of culture.

Romanticism was criticized for its manner of conceiving myth, as well as for its idea that the state is only a local expression of the universal Spirit, an idea that was considered to have later founded the totalitarianism of the twentieth century. However, Cassirer considers that romantic totalitarianism is not political, but is a cultural expression. Moreover, even if the perspective of the romantic spirit is always that of the Whole, then this totality does not exist independently from elements of that totality, namely from the individual existences that build the totality, and have the same right to exist as the Whole itself. The romanticists recognized the uniqueness of each nation, seen as a materialization of the universal Spirit. Romanticists embrace every such materialization of the universal Spirit, and their cultural totalitarianism strives to create an authentic form of spirituality, such as was the case with medieval Christianity, they being already conscious of its declining influence.

If German Romanticism was oriented towards myth and metaphysics, with the political realities being more a motive of contemplation than of action, then in Carlyle's work we find a shift in interest from metaphysics towards action, although a great part of the cultural paradigm of Romanticism was nevertheless taken over by him. Carlyle's conception of the hero presupposes both German Romanticism, with its cult of imagination and history, and Goethe's activism. Carlyle was a contemporary of Goethe. He knew German culture and was profoundly influenced by it. To him, romantic passion for history was no more than an occasion for contemplation that had lost its appeal. Already, Goethe saw this contemplation as being no longer an ideal. We may consider Goethe as being one of the first thinkers to have had a profound consciousness of the modern "crisis of values." He saw the absence of a true orientation of the spirit. This disorientation is well-described in his work, *Faust*, where the main character tried out everything and found no satisfaction, until he discovered that only action is able to satisfy the spirit, bringing him inner balance and harmony. Thus, Goethe expressed in his work a new value represented by action.

Even if the hero and the genius occupy a very important place in German Romanticism, we do not yet observe hero worship. In German culture, heroes, although exceptional figures, still remain exponents of the ever pervasive Absolute Spirit. On the other hand, in Carlyle, divinity has only a moral dimension and exists through the actions of outstanding individuals – heroes.

For Carlyle, Absolute Spirit no longer expresses itself through the whole of nature, but only through human nature and history. But, here only the hero reveals the intentions of divinity and is the real cause of the transformations of social and political life. Therefore, history remains a favorite domain for Carlyle. We must emphasize that the way of interpreting the role of the hero in revealing the intentions of divinity is not seen from the perspective of divinity, as in the metaphysical conception of Romanticism, but from that of the hero namely in an immanent mode, from the point of view of the intensity of the hero's faith. The hero becomes, according to Carlyle, an extraordinary man, not because he is considered in the context of divinity as being an instrument of the realization of the will and embodiment of God, but because he is considered from the point of view of his own moral force, of his inner power to impose on society and history his own ideals. This inner force makes the hero worthy of worship. The religious sentiment that was earlier oriented towards divinity has almost entirely vanished now or is at present merely a secularized religiousness. Therefore, notes Cassirer, "perhaps no other philosophical theory has done so much to prepare the way for the modern ideals of political leadership." (Cassirer 1946, 216)

In the nineteenth century, history was one of the disciplines that underwent very intense development, leading to a new self-consciousness of history, and to interrogation over its status as a science. How can we recognize history as a true science, and not merely an accumulation of historical knowledge lacking inner unity? Borrowing from the model of science, the principles of which are self-evident, and from which all the other contents of the science are deduced, Gobineau claimed that he succeeded in identifying a unique principle of history, the concept of race. In his theory about the differences between races, Gobineau affirms these differences to be fact (Cassirer 1946, 225), and in his opinion "fact" rendered the explanation for historical dynamic. Thus, in his theory, Gobineau reflected the fundamental concepts of his era, that realist and scientific thought of the nineteenth century, which searched in its theories for undoubted "facts," that were universally acknowledged.

The idea of the existence of race was not new; it had already appeared in the writings of Montesquieu. The novel perspective Gobineau brings is the value attributed to all races, especially to the white race, that is considered the very motor of history. All other values subordinated to this. The consequence was that every member of a "superior" race was, on account of the simple fact of its existence, superior not only to the members of other races but also to all creation belonging to that race. Therefore, in Cassirer's opinion, Gobineau's theory represented "an attempt to destroy all other values" (Cassirer 1946, 232). In introducing this new factor, Gobineau introduced into the historical discourse an irrational element in order to explain history and the state: the organization of the state, its power, and durability are grounded not on logical criteria, on a rational evaluation of the political decisions and acts, but are seen only as the expression of a substance that is the sole value, the unique entity that may explain and justify everything else. In this way, Gobineau reached a true "race worship" (Cassirer 1946, 245).

During the evolution of political conceptions that preceded and made possible the revival of myth within political thought, the philosophy of Hegel occupies, according to Cassirer, a very special place. His philosophy is treated in the final part of *The Myth of the State*, a special chapter being dedicated to him that disregards the historical order of the evolution of political philosophy. The totalitarianism of the twentieth century would not have been possible without the Hegelian conception. Here, we shall mention only a few of Hegel's ideas that were borrowed by totalitarianism. There is, Hegel says, a sense of history. This history is a dialectical process where we always meet conflict between opposites and their synthesis. Within history, Reason follows its own finality, independently from the intentions of human actors – we must emphasize that Reason is, according to Hegel, no more the Kantian reason (a human capacity of thinking), but a "Reason that lives in the historical world and organizes it" (Cassirer 1946, 258). By making Reason the grounds of reality, Hegel could claim that all that is real is also rational, and in this way legitimizing every action throughout history, however absurd and violent it seems. In history, this Reason acquires a concrete form through the reality of the state; different states being in reciprocal relationships that are necessarily full of tension. In a certain epoch, only one state can truly represent Reason or the universal Spirit. As an expression of the manifestation of the Idea of universal Spirit in history, the state is not an arbitrary existence but a necessary one. At the same time, it is not, according to Hegel, the result of a social contract but represents an organic unity where the whole precedes the parts. For Hegel, in contrast to other romanticists, this whole is tension-filled and materializes through the conflicts of its parts. Hegel does not accept the utopian representation of a condition where there are no conflicts between states or within a state, because this condition would ultimately lead to the death of the state itself. Thus, we see that Hegel also develops, in his political theory, the principle of his philosophy; according to this principle, Divinity (Reason) always means a) a self-dividing into opposites, b) their conflict, and c) their synthesis. Therefore, in spite of the "totalitarian" character of the state in the Hegelian conception – totalitarian because the metaphysical substance of the state precedes the reality of the individuals that built it –, in the end, individuals possess and attain here true signification and value. Here, individuals, with their passions and resulting conflicts, are the ones who materialize the state, and who give a concrete form to its substance within history. But they do this without knowing that they are actually only instruments of the "Cunning of Reason" in history.

Conclusions

We can now summarize the conceptual notes that were developed in the sphere of political thought throughout history, as presented by Cassirer in *The Myth of the State*, and about which he says that they are to be found in the conception of the state and of political action in the first half of the twentieth century. In this conception, first, there is a consciousness of the fact that the individual soul reflects the organization of the state (Plato). It is also the consciousness of a sense of history (Augustine). It can be said that this sense necessarily implies the apparition of the totalitarian state. Another note is that political action has an autonomous rationality (Thomas Aquinas) that may be transformed into a true technique (Machiavelli). All the effects of political action can be calculated, as in the mathematical science of nature (the philosophy of the seventeenth century). This action includes a practical realization of ideal representations (the Enlightenment), is supported by recourse to history and myth (the Romanticism), and is materialized around the hero, who is a messianic personality (the Romanticism and Carlyle). Finally, the state, from the point of view of the new Nazi myth, is the state of a superior race (Gobineau). Through the rational construction of this state the substance of race is expressed (Hegel). We observe how, throughout all these stages, reason is interwoven with myth. In his book, Cassirer shows that with each new stage in the development of reason, we encounter a metamorphosis of the mythical dimension, of religious thought. The mythical elements do not disappear in any conception, as rational as they would be. In all, we also find a mythical-religious dimension. But this dimension is so closely interwoven with reason that it appears almost to be unimportant. Thus, one has the impression that reason increasingly succeeds in dominating mythical thought, and that man transforms gradually into a true rational being for whom myth is only a bygone era of his own history. However, this turns out to be an illusion because myth can always come back in the present in a totally unexpected way for those who, as Cassirer states, have always believed in the ideal of reason:

"When we first heard of the political myths, says Cassirer, we found them so absurd and incongruous, so fantastic and ludicrous that we could hardly be prevailed upon to take them seriously. By now it has become clear to all of us that this was a great mistake." (Cassirer 1946, 296)

It is true that myth, as a "symbolic form", is opposed to reason because it is the result of a different form of synthesis of reality, and because it works with different mental categories. There is, thus, a logical opposition. However, there is also the idea that this opposition, besides being only a logical one, is also a temporal opposition in the sense that the apparition of reason in human history implies an abandonment of mythical thought, and that the two ways of thinking cannot exist simultaneously. Even Cassirer, as we saw, acknowledges that he was a victim of this illusion.

In the final pages of *The Myth of the State*, Cassirer cites Malinowski's interpretation, according to which primitive people are drawn to myth, and to instruments of the mythical thought, only in exceptional situations, namely in those situations that deviate from everyday logic and where the usual mode of thinking is inadequate. Hence, Cassirer acknowledges that reason and mythical thought can replace one another depending on the situation, and they simultaneously exist inside of the human being. He further applies this interpretation to his era in an attempt to explain the possibility of modern man, the so-called "rational" man, returning to mythical thinking. According to Cassirer, western society in the 1930s was in crisis, when the "collective wish" found no more its usual means of satisfaction and recourse to irrational means seemed to be unavoidable. The crisis was exactly that exceptional situation that ultimately led to the revival of myth. But western man does not absolutely transform himself into a primitive man this way; the presence of history cannot be eliminated in his being. Therefore, the political myth of the twentieth century can no longer be the myth of primitive man. It has a different content, one that is determined by the history of political conceptions. Myth is not an aberrant form. It has its logic. It is a form of organizing experience, and the product of a "classifying instinct" (Cassirer 1946, 15) specific to the human being. It is the "synthetic unity of a manifold", that, in the case of the political myth of the twentieth century, includes the whole history of political conceptions as well as the present critical situation of man. Myth, as Cassirer shows at the beginning of this book, is the result of an intense emotional experience. It opens a horizon, a new dimension inside of which it has evolution, its own history. The "barbarity" of coming back to this means of myth is not absolute. Modern man does not renounce at all what history has taught him, and does not become, in other words, a "primitive". This "barbarity" means only the pre-eminence in modern man, of another "classifying instinct" other than reason. His whole being, conditioned by the experience of history, remains the same, except that it acquires a new orientation. Thus, the merit of Cassirer's book is that it presents the components of the ideational manifold which is the foundation for the political myths of the twentieth century, components that developed, as we saw, during the millenary history of European spirit. These components do not exist in a disparate way, without any internal bound; rather, they determine one another and exist inside of an "order of foundation" and condition one another. Cassirer says in this sense:

"It is, however, clear that the personification of a collective wish cannot be satisfied in the same way by a great civilized nation as by a savage tribe. Civilized man is, of course, subject to the most violent passions, and when these passions reach their culminating point he is liable to yield to the most irrational impulses. Yet even in this case he cannot entirely forget or deny the demand of rationality. In order to believe he must find some ‚reasons' for his belief; he must form a 'theory' to justify his creeds. And this theory, at least, is not primitive; it is, on the contrary, highly sophisticated." (Cassirer 1946, 280-281)

The "collective wish" is not immediately objectified in modern man as it is in primitive man. Political myths do not appear spontaneously but are very elaborate and sophisticated products because they are founded upon knowledge. The synthesis with history presupposes that knowledge. While in primitive man, the rational reflection was not yet developed, modern man is precisely the result of such reflection. Even modern functionalism, the basis for science according to Cassirer, is the result of reflection. The reason for this is that in different disciplines of knowledge, concepts do not faithfully reflect reality; they do not appear on the grounds of perceived "resemblances" but are the results of reflective elaboration, of mental constructions. Political myths, as elaborated products, presuppose a good knowledge of man. They have the same finality as science does: manipulation. Modern sciences do not aim at "knowledge" for the sake of knowledge, but at the knowledge that permits the manipulation of reality, namely the transformation of it according to the goals of men; in the same way, the modern political myth takes advantage of this new orientation of the present spirit. Knowing that myth is a product of emotions, the creators of political myths appeal to such means by which the human emotions may be canalized in their interest:

"Myth has always been described as the result of an unconscious activity and as a free product of imagination. But here we find myth made according to plan. The new political myths do not grow up freely; they are not wild fruits of an exuberant imagination. They are artificial things fabricated by very skillful and cunning artisans. It has been reserved for the twentieth century, our own great technical age, to develop a new technique of myth. Henceforth myths can be manufactured in the same sense and according to the same methods as any other modern weapon – as machine guns or airplanes. That is a new thing – and a thing of crucial importance. It has changed the whole form of our social life." (Cassirer 1946, 282)

Thus, myth is not a symbolic form that was surpassed by the apparition and development of rational culture. Myth founds human culture, and the Babylonian myth of Marduk, cited by Cassirer at the end of his book, is used by him as an analogy for the fact that our entire culture is penetrated by myth, except in balanced epochs of history when mythical thought is tamed and lays in unity with other human faculties. During an era of crisis, mythical thought tends to occupy the foreground of the consciousness and impose itself on these faculties, or even overthrow all the value hierarchies that man has acquired in the course of his history. Although Cassirer admits the real worth of myth as an expression of the first form of objectification of the human spirit, for him, the myth still remains a primitive, undeveloped form of this objectification. Because myth is closely related to human sensibility, myth, mythical thought, and the type of imagination that is related to them represent true elemental forces of the human being, forces which we cannot directly oppose. Rather a pedagogical effort is needed to develop human capacity to avoid irrational fascination pertaining to those forces, by means of a true knowledge of the structures and mechanisms of mythical thought. If earlier in his investigations, Cassirer saw mythical thought as being only an object of scientific research, the revival of myth in his age made Cassirer consider this research as being an evaluation of a true adversary:

"We should carefully study the origin, the structure, the methods, and the technique of the political myths. We should see the adversary face to face in order to know how to combat him." (Cassirer 1946, 296)

Mythical thought can become an adversary for Cassirer only because this type of thinking eliminates human freedom. One of the features that define mythical thought is, according to Cassirer, the identity between the subject and the object of knowledge (Cassirer 2, 1977, 51; 82-85). Here we do not find any distance between thought and its object, a distance that is so necessary to rational thinking, and that only permits a free and responsible decision. On the contrary, this identification of the subject with the object leads to an action in which the subject is determined by the object, with actions being extensions and projections of the object inside the subject. In the context of new political myths, the totalitarian state is an object that imposes itself on the human subject, thereby striving to determine from within all his actions and kidnapping his freedom. The manipulation by these myths actually means the inculcation of the leader's will (who is thus identified with the state) in all members of the society, and their transformation in shades of his person.

In my opinion, the title of Cassirer's book has several meanings. The title refers to the fact that the concept of state in the Nazi era, and the era of the totalitarian state in general, proves a revival of certain features that belong to mythical thought. In this sense, we may understand the title, *The Myth of the State*, as describing the conditions of possibility pertaining to extremely complex myths with which the contemporaneous totalitarian state tries to legitimize itself. On the other hand, if we look also at the entire background of Cassirer's functionalistic thought, we may say that this book intends to prove, in a polemic way, the fact that the idea of the substance of state that would exist beyond history and be materialized by the totalitarian state is actually only fiction, in the negative meaning of the term, namely only a "myth". Finally, *The Myth of the State* indicates the extremely real peril (totally ignored until now) that, in totalitarian societies, the relationship between the state and its citizens may acquire a mythical character, thus losing its rational character. The state tends here, in other words, to depersonalize its citizens, to become the real subject of their subjectivity, and the center of their personality.

We must see in this last book of Ernst Cassirer the profession of faith of a great humanist, for whom reason, freedom, and culture are those values that raise the human being to the condition of true humanity.

References

- Cassirer, Ernst. 1923. *Substance and Function and Einstein's theory of relativity*. Chicago-London: The Open Court Publishing Company.

- Cassirer, Ernst. 1956. *Wesen und Wirkung des Symbolbegriffs*. Darmstadt: Wissenschaftliche Buchgesellschaft.

- Cassirer, Ernst. 1972. *An Essay on Man*, New Haven: Yale University Press.

- E. Cassirer. 1946 *The Myth of the State*, New Haven and London, Yale University Press.

- Cassirer, Ernst. 1977. *Philosophie der symbolischen Formen*, Erster Teil, *Die Sprache*. Darmstadt: Wissenschaftliche Buchgesellschaft.

- Cassirer, Ernst. 1977. *Philosophie der symbolischen Formen*, Zweiter Teil, *Das mythische Denken*, Wissenschaftliche Buchgesellschaft.

- Habermas, Jürgen. 2002. "The German Idealism of the Jewish Philosophers". In *Religion and Rationality: Essays on Reason, God, and Modernity*, ed. Eduardo Mendieta. Cambridge: MIT Press.

- Hamburg, C. H. 1949. "Cassirer's Conception of Philosophy". In *The Philosophy of Ernst Cassirer*, ed. P. A. Schilpp. Evanston, Illinois: The Library of Living Philosophers, Inc.

- Hamburg, C. H. 1964. "A Cassirer-Heidegger Seminar". In *Philosophy and Phenomenological Research*. 25, (2).

- Hegel, G. W. Fr. 1986. *Phänomenologie des Geistes*. Frankfurt am Main: Suhrkamp.

- Husserl, E. 1901. *Logische Untersuchungen*, Vol. II. Halle: Max Niemeyer.

- Görland, A. 1906. *Index zu Hermann Cohens Logik der reinen Erkenntnis*. Berlin: Verlag von Bruno Cassirer.

- Kant Immanuel. 1881. *Critique of pure reason*. First Part. Trans. F. Max Müller. London: Macmillan and Co.

- Kant Immanuel. 1881. *Critique of pure reason*. Second Part. Trans. F. Max Müller. London: Macmillan and Co.

Made in the USA
Middletown, DE
15 May 2021